A Sense of Science:
Exploring Sound

Claire Llewellyn

SEA-TO-SEA

Mankato Collingwood London

This edition first published in 2009 by
Sea-to-Sea Publications
Distributed by Black Rabbit Books
P.O. Box 3263
Mankato, Minnesota 56002

Printed in China

Library of Congress
Cataloging-in-Publication Data:

Llewellyn, Claire.
  Exploring sound / Claire Llewellyn.
    p. cm. -- (A sense of science)
  Summary: "A simple exploration of sound that
covers pitch, volume, hearing and ears, how humans
make sounds, and why animals make sounds.
Includes activities"--Provided by publisher.
  Includes index.
  ISBN 978-1-59771-133-3
  1. Sound--Juvenile literature. I. Title.
  QC225.5L64 2009
  534--dc22
                        2008007333

9 8 7 6 5 4 3 2

Published by arrangement with the
Watts Publishing Group Ltd, London.

Editor: Jeremy Smith
Art Director: Jonathan Hair
Design: Matthew Lilly
Cover and design concept:
Jonathan Hair
Photography: Ray Moller unless
otherwise stated.

Photograph credits:
Alamy: 6, 9b, 11b, 26, 27t.

We would like to thank Scallywags for
their help with the models in this book.

Contents

A world of sound

We hear all kinds of sounds in the world around us.

We hear children playing.

We hear traffic going by.

We even hear
the leaves
rustling on
the trees.

Sound play
Close your eyes and listen hard.
What can you hear right now?

Loud and soft

Sounds can
be loud
or soft.

Tick! Tock!

A ticking clock is very soft.

Tap, tap!
Tap a table to make a sound. First
make a soft sound. Then make a loud one.
What did you do to make it louder?

A road drill is very loud.

Warning!
Very loud
sounds can
hurt our
ears.

Ear muffs
protect our ears
from loud noise.

High and low

Sounds can
be high
or low.

Hummmm!
Hum a high note, and then a low
one. Do it again pressing your
thumb and finger against each side
of your throat. What can you feel?

A
triangle
makes a
very high
sound.

10

A tuba makes
a very
low sound.

Playing different instruments together
mixes up the sounds.

Our ears

We hear sounds
with our ears.

Warning!
Look after your
ears. Never put
small things
inside
them.

Ear

We all have
two ears, with
one on each side
of our head.

The shape of our ears helps pick up sounds.

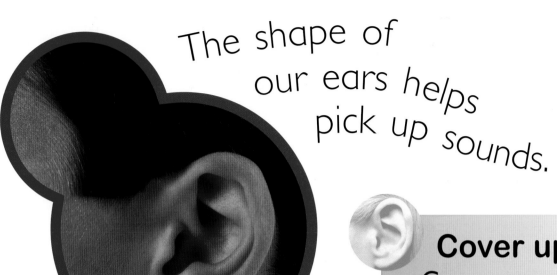

Cover up
Cover your ears with your hands. What do you notice?

Cupping a hand around our ears helps us hear even better.

Where's that sound?

We hear many different sounds at once. Our ears tell us where they are coming from.

Hear, hear

Ask a friend to whisper behind you. Then ask them to move farther away. Is it easier or harder to hear them now?

Our ears can tell us if a sound is far away ...

...or if it is nearby.

Making sounds

We make musical sounds in different ways.

Shake Shake
Find two empty yogurt cartons. Put some sugar in one, and some beads in the other. Shake them. Are the sounds the same?

Blowing into a recorder makes a whistling sound.

Shaking maracas makes a sound like a rattle.

We can make tapping sound on a drum.

Our body makes sounds

Our body makes many different sounds.

Sometimes our stomach grumbles when we are hungry!

We can make a
sound by snapping
our fingers.

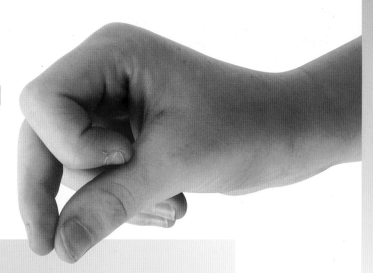

Body sounds
Try making three sounds with different
parts of your body. Which is the loudest
sound? Which is the softest?

We can
clap our
hands loudly
or softly.

We can speak!

We can make sounds with our voice.

We can talk and listen to each other.

We make music when we sing.

Speak up!
Ask three friends to stand behind you. Then ask them to each say "Hello." Can you tell who is speaking each time?

Everyone's voice is a little bit different.

21

Hard to hear

Deaf people cannot hear well.
Some of them need
a hearing aid to
hear what people
are saying.

Many deaf people also learn to read people's lips.

Cover up

Ask someone to talk to you with their hand over their mouth. Is it harder to understand them if you can't see their lips?

Some people learn to use hand signs, too.

Animals and sound

Hearing helps keep
animals safe.

Hares have big
ears and are always listening
for danger.

A lamb finds its mother by listening for her call.

A cat's ears help it catch mice in the dark.

In the dark

Listen hard when you go to bed. Can you hear any animals in the night? What are they?

Staying safe

Our hearing helps
to keep us safe.

If we hear a dog
growl, we stay
away from it.

If we hear a fire alarm, we can save ourselves from a fire.

Danger, danger
What kind of noise could you make if you were in danger and needed help?

Rrring! Rrring!

A bicycle bell warns people to get out of the way.

Glossary

Deaf
Cannot hear well.

Double bass
A musical instrument that looks like a big violin. It makes a very low sound.

Hand sign
A way of "talking" to deaf people by moving your hands.

Hearing aid
A little machine worn behind the ear that helps deaf people hear.
Musical instrument
Something that makes a musical sound, like a recorder.

Recorder
A musical instrument with a wooden tube and holes for the fingers.

Voice
The sound made by a person when she or he speaks or sings.

Make a sound box

Here's a game to play with a friend.

1. Find a cardboard box with a lid.

2. Take turns collecting small objects from around the house, such as a cork, a marble, or some dried beans.

3. Then hide the things inside the box, one at a time.

4. Can your friend guess what's inside the box when you shake it?

Index